DIGGING UP DINOSAUR FOSSILS IN

ASIA

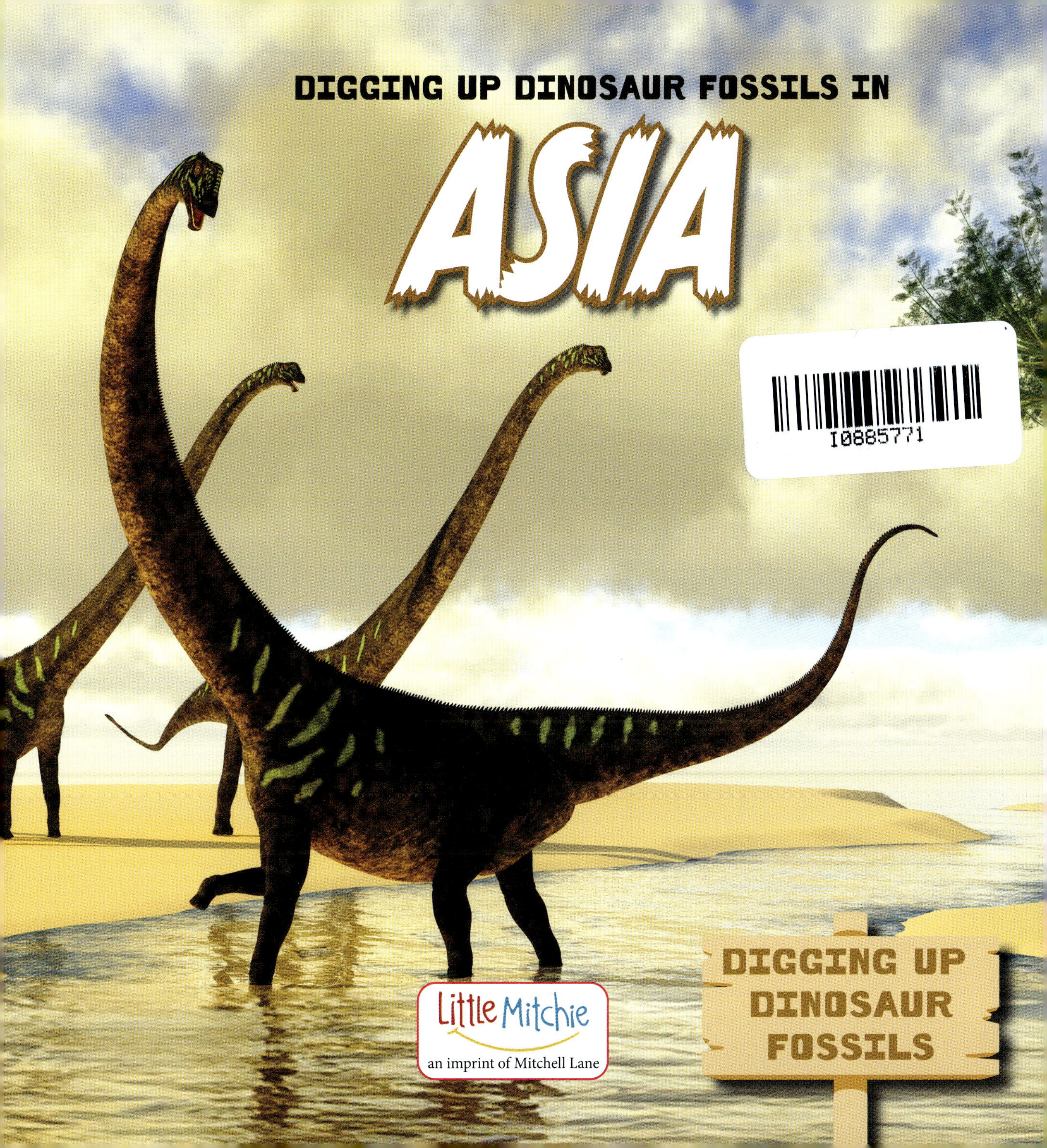

DIGGING UP DINOSAUR FOSSILS

Little Mitchie
an imprint of Mitchell Lane

Creating Young Nonfiction Readers

***Little Mitchie* lets children delve into nonfiction at beginning reading levels. Young readers are introduced to new concepts, facts, ideas, and vocabulary.**

Tips for Reading Nonfiction with Young Readers

Talk about Nonfiction

Begin by explaining that nonfiction books give us information that is true. The book will be organized around a specific topic or idea, and we may learn new facts through reading.

Look at the Parts

Most nonfiction books have helpful features. Our *Little Mitchie* titles include color photographs and graphic aids, a table of contents, a glossary, and an index. Share the purpose of these features with your reader.

Color Photos and Graphic Aids

A lot of information can be found by "reading" photos, charts, maps, and other graphic aids found within nonfiction texts. Help your reader learn more about the different ways information can be displayed.

Table of Contents

Located at the front of the book, this list shows the big ideas within the text and the page numbers where they can be found.

Glossary

Located at the back of the book, the glossary defines key words and phrases that are related to the topic. These words and phrases can be found in the text in colored type.

Index

Located at the back of the book, an index is an alphabetical list of topics and the page numbers where they can be found.

With a little help and guidance about reading nonfiction, you can feel good about introducing a young reader to the world of *Little Mitchie* nonfiction books.

Mitchell Lane
PUBLISHERS

2001 SW 31st Avenue
Hallandale, FL 33009
www.mitchelllanepub.com

Little Mitchie

First Edition, 2025.

Author: Meg Greve
Designer: Rhea Magaro
Editor: Madison Greve

Names/credits:
Title: Digging Up Dinosaur Fossils in Asia / by Meg Greve
Description: Hallandale, FL :
Mitchell Lane Publishers, [2025]

Series: Digging Up Dinosaur Fossils
Library bound ISBN: 979-8-89260-239-6
Paperback ISBN: 979-8-89260-416-1
eBook ISBN: 979-8-89260-248-8

Little Mitchie is an imprint of
Mitchell Lane Publishers.

PHOTO CREDITS
Alamy: Stocktrek Images, Inc., 8-9; Mohamad Haghani, 14-15; Ivan Vdovin, 16-17; Aleksei Gorodenkov, 20-21; Shutterstock: Catmando, cover, 1; Colorcocktail, cover, 1 (sign); kamomeen, 3; Aust28, 4, 6, 9, 11, 13, 15, 17, 18, 20, 23; Noiel, 5; Natalia van D, 6-7; Daniel Eskridge, 10-11; Elenarts, 12-13; Catmando, 18-19

CONTENTS

When Dinosaurs Ruled the Land

More than 200 million years ago, the first dinosaurs hatched on Earth. They ate plants that grew all around them and sometimes each other. The world was warmer than it is now. This was Asia before it was a **continent**. This was the time of the dinosaurs!

Before there were seven continents, all land formed one giant continent called Pangea.

Paleontologists are scientists who find and study dinosaur fossils. These **fossils** show us what Asia may have looked like millions of years ago. Let's learn about some Asian dinosaurs!

DINO DETAILS:
Dinosaurs who hunted other animals often had strong, powerful legs for running and attacking.

Meat for Dinner? Meet the Carnivores!

Sinraptor was a vicious **carnivore.** It had front teeth that could crush bones and back teeth for ripping flesh. It was able to take down dinosaurs much bigger than itself!

DINO DETAILS:
Dinosaurs could not fly until there were true birds. But many of them may have been covered in soft feathers like today's birds.

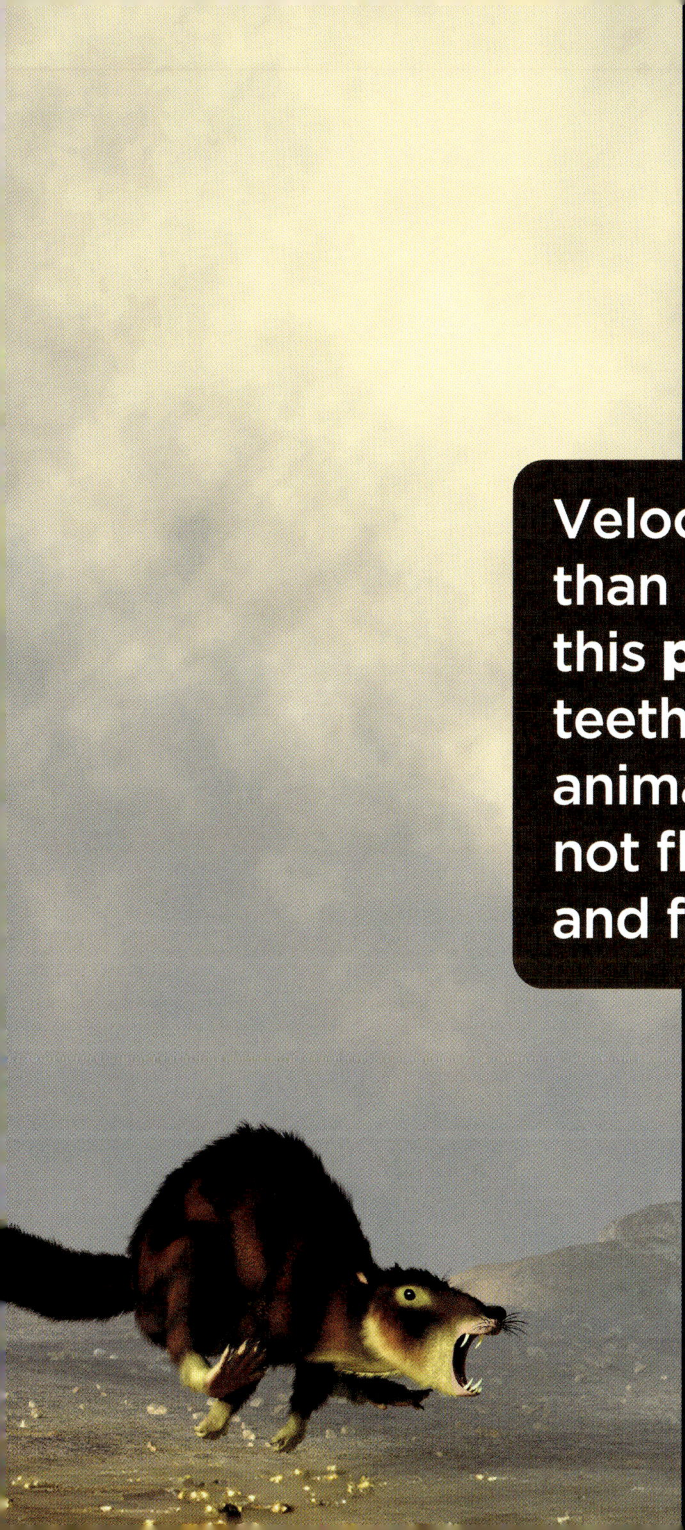

Velociraptor was smaller than an adult human. But this **predator** had about 80 teeth it used to eat smaller animals. Velociraptor could not fly, but it did have wings and feathers!

DINO DETAILS:
All relatives of the tyrannosaurs had short arms that were not used for walking or running.

Alioramus was a relative of Tyrannosaurus rex. It was smaller, so it ate smaller **prey**. It also had small horns and bumps on its head to attract mates.

DINO DETAILS:
Paleontologists do not find complete skeletons very often. But the skeleton of Shunosaurus comes very close.

More Plants for the Herbivores, Please!

Shunosaurus had a small skull with small teeth. This **herbivore** had a long neck to reach leaves on the tops of trees. It also had a bony club at the end of its long tail.

DINO DETAILS:
There was a group of dinosaurs that had frills, horns, and domes. These could be used to find a mate or scare away enemies.

Protoceratops had a frill at the back of its neck. It grew bigger as the dinosaur grew older. It had slim legs but was not a fast runner.

Mamenchisaurus had one of the longest necks of any dinosaur. It was not able to raise its head above its shoulders. Instead, it would swing its head back and forth to eat plants close to the ground.

DINO DETAILS:
Some dinosaurs with longer necks used them to reach the highest parts of trees. Some used them for grazing plants low to the ground.

Millions of years ago, Asia looked much different than it does today. By studying Asian dinosaur fossils, we can see into the history of Asia and the world we live in today.

Where Did the Dinosaurs Live?

- **Alioramus:** Mongolia
- **Mamenchisaurus:** China (East Asia)
- **Protoceratops:** Mongolia and China
- **Sinraptor:** China (Xinjiang and Sichuan)
- **Shunosaurus:** China (Sichuan)
- **Velociraptor:** Mongolia (Gobi Desert)

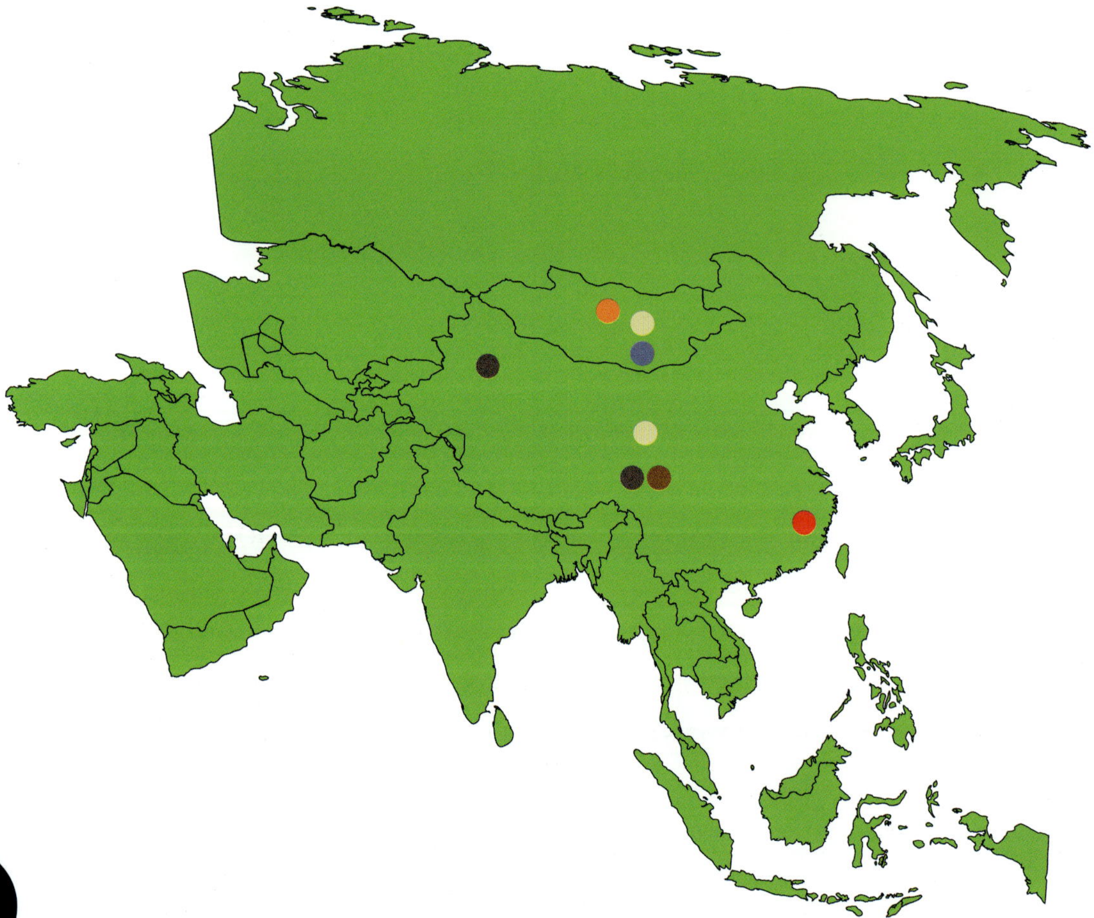

Interesting Facts

- The word dinosaur means "terrible lizard."
- Many dinosaurs may have been covered in feathers.
- About 66 million years ago, a huge asteroid crashed into Earth that killed off all dinosaurs except for birds.
- Some dinosaurs cared for their young, while other dinosaurs left their young to survive on their own.
- Some dinosaurs had crests on their heads that are like the wattles on some birds.

Spotlight On: Xu Xing

Xu Xing has named more dinosaurs than any other paleontologist on Earth. He thinks he has named about 80 but cannot remember the exact number. One area of interest for him is evolution. Xing studies how dinosaurs evolved into the modern birds we know today. When Xing went to college, he had not ever heard the words paleontologist or dinosaur. But through his studies and travels, he discovered his interest in fossils. This interest has not yet stopped. He continues to search for the next dinosaur fossil to add to his collection.

Glossary

carnivore (KAR-ni-vor):
A meat-eating animal

continent (KON-tin-ent):
One of the seven largest pieces of land on Earth

fossils (FAH-suhls):
Rock that forms after a living thing is preserved in the earth

herbivore (ER-buh-vor):
A plant-eating animal

predator (PRE-duh-ter):
An animal that hunts other animals for food

prey (pray):
Animals hunted and eaten by other animals

Index

Further Reading

Arlon, Penny. *My First Dinosaur Atlas: Roar Around the World with the Mightiest Beasts Ever!*. San Francisco, CA: Weldon Owen, 2022.

Hansen, Grace. *Dinosaur Graveyards in Asia*. Minneapolis, MN: Abdo Books, 2021.

Leed, Percy. *The Mighty Velociraptor*. Minneapolis, MN: Lerner Publications, 2022.

On the Internet

Velociraptor
https://kids.nationalgeographic.com/animals/prehistoric/facts/velociraptor
Learn lots of facts about the fierce Velociraptor.

Dinosaurs: Tour a Dinosaur Lab
https://sciencetrek.org/topics/dinosaurs
Watch a tour of a dinosaur lab and learn facts about dinosaurs.